WANTED

Tiffany Anne Tondut is a neurodivergent poet and artist living in London. She was a winner of the inaugural Poetry Archive Now! Wordview 2020 competition, and a winner of the Troubadour International Poetry Prize 2015. Her work has been broadcast, commissioned, exhibited, anthologised and published in a number of publications including *The Rialto, Magma, The Guardian Online* and *Best British and Irish Poets.* In 2015, she founded poetry press Laudanum. Tiffany has taught both written and performance poetry for The City Lit, and performed for The Festival of Britain and National Theatre Wales. Her debut chapbook *The God of Love is Stained* was published by Silkworms Ink in 2013.

ISBN: 978-1-915760-01-2

Cover designed by Aaron Kent

Edited & Typeset by Aaron Kent

Broken Sleep Books Ltd
Rhydwen
Talgarreg
Ceredigion
SA44 4HB

Broken Sleep Books Ltd
Fair View
St Georges Road
Cornwall
PL26 7YH

Brutal, unsettling and yet seductive. Reading these poems feels like watching a great film in which the heroine shape-shifts refusing to be identified as any one woman – at once femme fetale, factory girl, windswept ingenue, grieving daughter, and contemporary lover side-eyeing the camera with a healthy dose of irony. Death, sex and cashmere… what more could you ask for?

— Ella Frears, *Shine Darling*

The poems of *Wanted* are stylish in the enduring way of the very best poetry, and they are substantial. Their substance is language and history, always personal, whether the simulacrum of a love affair or the lot of the canary girls and their children in the Second World War. Their substance is life's crucial landscapes of love and death seen through literature and visual art. Their style virtuosically transfigures substance in a new language.

— Kimberly Campanello, *Mother Baby Home*

These vignettes of contested memories, and stories lurking behind stories, are pin-sharp when it comes to the moments that matter: the ones that linger. *Wanted* has the air of the last cigarette you know you shouldn't smoke, but my god it's worth it.

— Rishi Dastidar, *Ticker Tape*

Wanted lives up to its title – addictive, obsessional and dangerous. The collection fizzes with great titles that are tart and compelling, plunging the reader on a passionate love affair with poems inhabited by protagonists from art, literature, and myth. Tondut's handling of colour and image, and boldness of address are exceptional. These are poems that get under the skin and electrify the blood, making your heart beat that bit faster, echoing the sharp pace of Tondut's cracking lines and her sublime feel for drama. If a bullet through the heart is implicit, it is faced with attitude. Dorothy Parker's spirit is conjured in poems alive with wit and bravado that are not afraid to take a risk and push language off the white cliff of a line-break. Formally and linguistically inventive, Tondut's debut pamphlet is as exciting as it is sensual, with a feminist core, which leaves the reader buoyed and ready for any showdown.

— Lisa Kelly, *A Map Towards Fluency*

Contents

Wanted

Tiffany Anne Tondut

For Margot, Little Miss Outlaw

I can only write a poem if it has some form of punishment in it...

— Chelsey Minnis

Leaves, after Lucian Freud

Don't read me the way you read Lucian's art,
half-arsed, *it's a girl with a plant.*

Stumble on colour, perspective, light.
Say *I don't get her, but want to.*

Forget about colour, perspective, light.
Close the damn book, try something like:

*the way he painted those leaves about her hair
you can tell he must have loved her.*

Floodlights

i promised to write about your black jeans
but then I read *an almost made up poem*
by charles bukowski. bukowski and his girl
wrote letters back and forth
but that was in the 70s. i guess i could write
you paper letters, then at least we could touch
the same sheets. bukowski's girl wrote poems
about angels and god in capitals. the poems i
type for you are in lower case, but bold.
i've hung out with famous artists, but unlike her
only some were my lovers. you're ok with who
i'm dating because we haven't met. you text:
i hope he treats you like the diamond that you are.
he didn't. i realise men who touch me
must disappear. one night, you leave me
a voicemail about a sandwich. your drunk
accent made me laugh with pain. i wanted more.
i know i'm not the best female poet on the scene
but maybe you think i am, and i love you
like a woman loves a man she's never met.
i know i'd love you more touching
your black jeans, stroking your nude back saying
"remember floodlights on our skin?"
but that hasn't happened. perhaps it never will
and my poems will sadden. men
will keep forgetting me or worse – i'll meet
a nice enough guy and never write you again.
i don't have a bench near a bridge over
a river where i go at night to weep,
but that doesn't mean i don't think of going there.
in three or four months i hope i've met you
and i don't care if you're unfair to me.
i'll be unfair to you.

This Man Comes in

He's tough, this man. A worker. Early. Shoulders the weight
of a high-rise day, boots brick-heavy, hands – gloveless,
       calloused.

"Better to grip" he'd wink, rolling a smoke for a fix on the go
as he waves in trucks, cranes, deliveries of rain to a roof
       where he weighs up the wind.

For him, the clearest threat was glass; fear was a pipe burst.
Now there's a risk that's more than the building's worth
       and when this man comes in

he's drilling what-ifs through his head, numbers, equipment,
boundaries unheeded by men and we touch, but after
       he's showered.

       And after he's showered,
after I've massaged the hours from out his back or legs,
I think about clapping, look to the clock and realise, again,
       what we've missed.

The God of Love is Stained

What's more, he's miserable.
One hundred and forty years
he's endured the same woman

clutching his arm, hoping
in some small human way
he'll bless her, alter her life

for the better. But I sense
she's secretly waiting for me
to fling the rock of my fist

through their pane, shattering
light, shattering love,
or that which appears to be.

Inspired by 'The God of Love and Alceste' stained glass window
designed by Edward Burne-Jones for William Morris, 1861-64

Canary Girls

i.m. 'The Canary Girls' of Munitions Factories 1914-1918

No machine had ever felt the plumage of a girl.
No girl had ever flown inside the cabin of a crane
and worked it.

News broke swift – fields of houses emptied.
Whole factories beating deft with women's wings.

Every flock had tools to ply:
some hammered, quick as beaks; others preened steel
or weighed and measured, nursing bombs
with a mother's eye.

New girls hatched in night shifts –
faces bright as yolk from packing shells with TNT.

Feathers erupted – streaks of fire through skin.
Some girls burned, blew away.

Canary Babies

'nearly every baby was born yellow'

Those months we laboured away
were bitter. Powder. TNT.

A million shells a week we filled,
yellowing. Hair bleached.

We sang through shifts to lift us.
A doctor came. He warned us not to work

with mouths open.
You birds'll give birth to canaries he joked

deadpan. Stethoscope.
The stain will fade said nurses

but I was branded, yellow-eyed.
First I saw the bird, then the child.

Canary Mother

You are kissing. You
        are kissing   her hands,
her tiny feet,
her face.   Your blindness.
        Stumped
arms.
Your lips untouched by the blaze.

The Last Darling

Rare as an orange footman or a silver-studded blue,
a *darling* fluttered out from his mouth.

Unlike "my darling," or those that used to utter
through openings of doors, this specimen was drab,

stranger than before, and she clapped it to her breast;
her hands, handkerchiefs, unfolding.

Cashmere

I bought a cashmere jumper.
It's just a scrap. A handkerchief. A wisp
of cashmere darling, you know I don't indulge.

You should have seen me walking out
with it draped over my arm. I must have looked quite smug –
but this is what age and money affords you:
Independence. Chicken. Cashmere.

You can't even afford your own cream.
I had to buy you that, for your athlete's foot.
This is what you're leaving sweetie, and when that tube runs out
you'll come crawling back.

And who picked out that slinky top?
Who knew what sexy was? I did. I dressed you
for that interview and you got it. You're a P.T because of me.

It's just a dash darling, but you know what they say...
women who wear cashmere don't need anyone.

Wuthering

a were gypsy, loose as orse:
aughty, ungry, nobody's flame;
are-bell eyes, slew as curse.

a thought e wouldn't want me, bu e did.

e drove me oop t'heath fer windswept walks.
we parked, fidgeted, talked.

e said a smelt of life,
is valley girl.
a named im darkling –
pupils so black, stars could sink.

a loved the damage in is grin
an the danger.
e loved me wild, bu couldn't let me go.
oft-times e buckled, gripped, slipped –
called me philistine, o bitch.

a writhed.
e said a needed taming.
a reared.
e brought a riding crop.
a howled.
e broke me in.

a thought *e cannot kill me*. bu e did.

O the patient ladies;
the ladies playing patience.

The shuffling and the pacing.
Windows draped with women waiting.

O the patient ladies; the playing of patience.

That breathless weather when nothing stirs,
no post delivered, no stamp of horse.

O the patient ladies; the ladies playing.

Dull needle – suspense of thread.
Proposals from unwanted men.

O the patient ladies; the ladies playing ladies.

Heaviness of bed;
doctors with powders for panting breasts.

O the ladies playing patients.

Wanted

on dead days
like this i wish
i was dillinger
s moll draped
in fox fur workin
g a stick of red
against my lips
chewin
g gum with an
american accent
him in his chalk line
d suit stiff
muscular hair
broad cuffs an
d brogues poundin
g up town my
long legs matchin
g the swing of
his gun hell
just knowin
g he killed
all those people
& not me?
that's what i call love.

Catullus 75

Huc est mens deducta tua, mea Lesbia, culpa,
Atque ita se officio perditit ipsa suo,
Ut iam nec bene velle queat tibi, si optuma fias,
Nec desistere amare, Omnia si facias.

Here's the thing – you've fucked me up Lesbia,
Though I'll admit I've screwed myself by loving you.
So I cannot wish you well, should you reach your premium,
Nor give up loving, if all you're worth is nil.

If Lesbia Could Reply:

Reply? Why should I. He's a twat.

Juice

My lover leaves me lemon juice so bitter
it stings to see its sour light, his remedy.

And still, I swallow it – bite with gratitude –
knowing he carved and pressed and poured

my health, like every morning spent, absent,
when I've been half at sleep

still holding onto a dream, unaware
of his hands, sharp, already in the kitchen.

Sex is a Bitch from Heaven

with hands of nails
cigarette nipples
teeth that bite
thru babies

eyes like canons
my hunter green eyes

i prefer champagne
revolver red
wine shipwrecks
death cars and duende excite me

it's not you i'm into
i'd sooner have school boys
with hazelnut hair

eyes like canons
my hunter green eyes

the bin is blooming with durex
supposedly numbing
the walls of my
bedroom are venus white
alex is gun smoke
ollie is pale swan
(but henry stayed in brighton)
i've got windows the colour of outer space
venus bedroom
dull virtuous moon

eyes like canons
my hunter green eyes

my father had false teeth

and one drunk night near the death
of his married life
he crawled into my
room crying forgive me
you won't see me again
like this

and henry might yet still come
pale swan is coming tomorrow
but gun smoke is coming any minute now

eyes like canons
my hunter green eyes

Lilies, by David Hockney

I wanted my father to die.
He was in the oncology ward: collapsed lung,
Stage IV.

Your father's awake and he wants to see you.
That was Tuesday. By Friday he was sitting up,
joking, tipping the nurse.

I took her outside.
"He's dying" she assured me, "it's just a final surge."
At last, I could sigh. Here's death.

Shotgun Wedding

as bonnie &
clyde swerve
d the deluxe ford
sedan between
deep rows of
louisiana pine
in bienville parish
they were married
thru their bodies
by the same bullets
texan officers emp
tied 24 guns on
the couple one
hundred & thirty
rounds of steel
jacket shells ham
mered out what
sounds like fitz
gerald scatting
how high the moon
& after the pair
were blown a
way those bullets
kept them dancing
in their seats

Don't Tell the Bride

The aisle is a wire between two cliffs.
The aisle is a roller-coaster.
The aisle is a plank.
The aisle is a beach.
The aisle's too dark
to walk down
without
glow-sticks.

It isn't what she—
She thought she—
He knows her better than—
She understands his—
When she saw him—
When she heard him—
He told her—
At the end of the day.

This is the Goddess Poem

These arms or no arms.
These breasts or no breasts.
These legs or no legs.

Embrace them.

These arms have earned money.
These words have earned money.
It's these words or no words.

Embrace them

Acknowledgements

Thank you to the editors of the following publications and exhibitions in which some of these poems, or versions of them, first appeared: *Bad Kid Catullus* (Sidekick Books), *Best New British and Irish Poets* (Eyewear Publishing, 2016), *Healing Words - The Advocacy Project, Magma, The E-List, The Moth, Poetry Trail Anthology 2012, The Rialto, South Bank Poetry, Vanguard Editions, Walthamstow Forest Echo, William Morris Gallery, York Literary Review*.

'The Last Darling' was a winner in the Troubadour International Poetry Prize, 2015.

'This Man Comes In' was a winner of the inaugural Poetry Archive Now! Wordview: 2020 competition

Thank you to my dear family and friends for your support over the past decade during which these poems were written, especially my beautiful mother - outlaw, supertramp, trailblazer.

LAY OUT YOUR UNREST

www.ingramcontent.com/pod-product-compliance
Lightning Source LLC
Chambersburg PA
CBHW021948040426
42448CB00008B/1297